GRIGGY'S NEW UNIVERSAL MAHJONG

By Richard T Weston & Pauline Day

©2018 All Rights Reserved

ISBN 9780995617285

Language: American English.

1st Edition February 2019 v1.02

Mahjong need not be difficult to learn, and Griggy's proves this. While retaining forty-four challenging hands, all the, previously difficult, scoring has been done for you. Instructions reduced to include only the essential elements that enhance the game. The result is a faster, more skill-based game that should encourage greater numbers to play and enjoy this fascinating game.

Though this guide references the works of Max Robertson and many others, it presents a significant enhancement and complete reassessment of all earlier guides.

Much simplified, Griggy's New Universal Mahjong, aims to both encourage a new generation to play this incredibly addictive game by providing a tested, universally acceptable and balanced scoring system.

Why this new guide?

My good friend, Pauline Day had played 'Mah Jong' for five decades with a group of friends who have all now moved on or passed away. Missing the game terribly, Pauline (Griggy to her friends), nagged and badgered me, her Grandchildren and anyone else who came near, to learn to play. The years passed and eventually, four of us agreed to try to learn and play this fascinating game.

We all struggled to grasp the game from Max Robertson's, very word-heavy, 'The Game of Mah Jong'. With Pauline herself, having to reference this guide continually, we all began to question its usefulness. The very dated guide lacked good formatting, pictorial examples and included an extremely complex method of scoring (especially fishing hands). Even finding a hand that we knew was a challenge. The internet was no help either; every set of instructions had its own, often muddled explanation or reverted to a simple Chinese Pung and Kongs only game.

We battled on, but our new player's interest was faltering as so much time was wasted trying to score hands and work out fishing scores. We discovered gross unfairness too: A player building a complete and difficult hand (a Mah Jong) might score 1000, where an opponent, who was fishing (one tile short of a Mah Jong) for a simpler hand could, with the pure luck of picking up some flowers, could score well over 10,000.

While accepting that luck should play a part in Mahjong, the scoring system had evolved into a system that was unnecessarily complex, and that rewarded luck more than it did a player's skill. Also, our tiring new players found it difficult to learn and remember all the different hands. We needed a way to find hands that matched the tiles in our racks.

I have always been a problem solver, finding methods to overcome my dyslexia being an early example. I could see glimpses of a great game beneath the rules and strange scoring system and set about bringing the game back to the surface.

Griggy's Universal Mahjong was created. Initially, it was just a set of photographs – Hand Cards - examples of all the different hands that we could flick through to find or check the requirements of a hand. These photographs worked quite well, except that they would get shuffled and they didn't help with fishing hand scoring.

When comparing and sorting the Hand Cards, the unfairness and the almost random way that the hands were scored became apparent. So, in 2018, I began to devise a completely new system, using the elements of each hand to calculate its value. While this is a complex formula, the players and readers of this guide, do not need to understand it.

Each Hand Card simply displays the resulting score for a Mah Jong (two and four player game) and the score it gives for those fishing for it. Simple – and no more hunting through a guidebook at the end of each round.

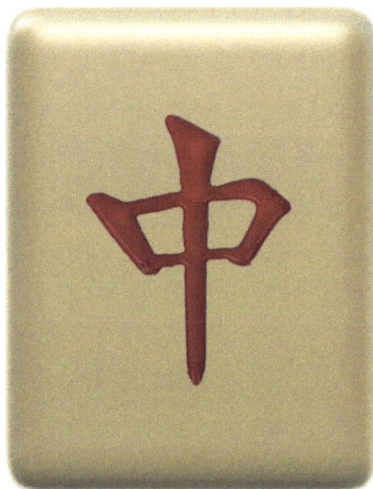

Apologies to my fellow UK readers: I have written this guide in American English because the market for this book is much greater in the US. I ask you to please put up with 'color', 'favorite', the odd 'Z' where you would expect an 'S' as well as a few extra commas.

Your Mahjong Set

To play Mahjong, you need to have a set of the most commonly used tiles – that of 'American Mahjong' also referred to as 'Mah-Jongg' in the US.

Is it Mah Jong or Mahjong?

We'd better clear this up early: The original spelling was *Mah Jong,* but the accepted spelling for the game is now Mahjong. Griggy's takes advantage of these different spellings: We use the spelling 'Mahjong' for the name of the game and 'Mah Jong' for a completed hand. In other words, **"Today, I am going to learn how to play Mahjong. When I complete a hand in Mahjong, I will call *Mah Jong!*"**

American Mahjong is the most skill based and widely adopted version of the game, played across Great Britain, Europe and America. Unfortunately, it has also devolved into several different versions with different images on the tiles as well as differing hands and rules — many, so complex that those new to the game often abandon it. But wait up! – Griggy's New Universal Mahjong isn't complicated, is the easiest to learn and still retains the fun element by rewarding skills you can quickly gain.

What's in the box?

There are a total of 144 tiles in a set (Leave any completely blank (spares) or 'joker' tiles in the box).

There are four of each of thirty-four different tiles. These tiles are used to create hands. There are also flowers - tiles that are not used within hands except Heavenly Paradise which is exceptionally rare!

Twenty-seven of these tiles belong to the three Suits: Bamboo*, Circles** and Characters. There are four of each of these suit tiles, and these are numbered one to nine. The Bamboo tiles are also divided into red and green - Colors that are specified in some of the hands.

There are three Dragons - Red, White, and Green, again, four of each. Beware the white Dragons are usually depicted as blank tiles – don't leave your White Dragons in the box!

Then, there are the Winds: Four of each – East, North, West, and South.

Finally, there are the flowers – 2 sets numbered 1 to 4 – One with Red numbers, one with Black. A complete set (1 to 4) of the same color are known as a Bouquet. Caution: I have found a set where one set of flowers were named, and the others called 'seasons.'. However, for simplicity, I refer to them as Red and Black sets of flowers. See photo on the next page for variations.

**The Bamboo tiles are sometimes also referred to as Sticks, Poles or Lines.

*Circle tiles are sometimes also referred to as Stones, Spots, Dots and Cookies.

Also, in your set, you should have four racks for concealing your tiles from other players, a pair of dice and a set of four Wind of the Round markers. One of the racks is different, usually having a black back. This rack is referred to as the 'marked rack' and is given to the East Wind Player – The player who starts the game. We refer to the East Wind player as *EAST*, for simplicity.

You may also find counters or 'chips' and complicated looking doubling tables, but, don't worry, we won't be needing those. Griggy's Guide does not include gambling instructions; we consider Mahjong as a fun game that doesn't lend itself well to betting. The doubling tables are not required either because the hand cards display all the majority of the scores.

You will also require a notepad and a pen to record the scores.

Below you can see some of the variations between 'standard' sets.

The top row shows all One's of Bamboo. Don't confuse these with flowers.

Note the very different 'Chinese' symbols on the Characters (3rd row down)

Glossary of Terms

The Stuff every player needs to know

Those who have played Mahjong previously can probably skip this section.

For those new to Mahjong, it would be helpful to know some terms and new words that are associated with the game. While each Hand Card (Page 24) does explain many of these, it is best to be familiar with the following.

The Wall – Tiles placed face down in a square – two rows high - 18 tiles per side. Once the wall is broken (Page 10 Start Playing), tiles are then taken from the anti-clockwise end during normal play.

Loose Tiles – 2x Tiles placed, face down on the far (clockwise) end of the wall. These are replaced from the same end of the wall as they are taken.

Your Rack – This is where you place your tiles so that only you can see and sort them. Tiles on your rack are **Concealed.**

EAST- The player who starts the round,

Marked Rack – The rack used to identify *EAST*

Exposed / Revealed Tiles – Any tiles laid face up so all players can see them.

Concealed hand / Tiles – Elements that remain on your rack or hands made entirely from tiles from the wall.

Discards – Tiles you and your opponent/s have discarded from the rack. Usually unwanted, these tiles are laid face-up in the middle of the wall with the discarding player announcing their name as they do so.

Dead Tiles- Tiles discarded by players not wanting them, that are not claimed by any other player before the next player takes their turn

Elements: Groups of tiles that are used to construct hands. These are Runs, Chows, Pungs, Kongs, Pairs or Knitting – See the following page for the full explanation.

Hands – Groups of Elements collected to form any one of the forty-four hands.

Mah Jong – The first player to complete any of the hands calls 'Mah Jong!' winning the round and scoring that hand's Mah Jong score. See the appropriate Hand Card.

Round- Games are played by completing rounds. A Round ends when, either a player calls "Mah Jong!" or the wall runs out of tiles.

Goulash- A round that ends without any player completing a hand.

Buried Treasure – Buried Treasure is not a hand. It is a bonus applied to some hands if the hand is completed fully concealed (without picking up any Discards). The Hand Cards state if it applies with a buried treasure symbol. Buried Treasure does not affect Fishing scores.

Fishing – If any player only requires one tile to complete a hand, they are fishing. Players who are fishing should clearly announce this to the other players. Players who are Fishing when another calls "Mah Jong!" each receive the 'Fishing Score' – This is marked on each Hand Card and is usually equal to half the full Mah Jong score.

Honours – The Honour tiles are the Winds, Dragons and all Suit tiles numbered either One or Nine.

THE ELEMENTS

All Mahjong hands are made up of Elements.

Those familiar with the game may skip this section. Speed readers can read just the bold and underlined text.

PAIR – Any <u>Two identical</u> tiles

KNITTED PAIR – <u>Two tiles</u> with the <u>same number</u> but from <u>different suits</u>

KNITTING – <u>Three tiles</u> with the <u>same number</u>, one from each of the suits

PUNG – Any <u>three matching</u> tiles

CHOW – A <u>Run</u> of just <u>three tiles</u> from the <u>same suit.</u> A Run means having sequential numbers, e.g., 7-8-9, etc. Except for the hand Windy Chows, only one Chow is permitted in a hand.

FULL RUN – A Run from <u>1 to 9</u> in the <u>same suit.</u>

Specified Run – Some hands require <u>specific ranges of numbers</u> from the <u>same suit.</u> Gates of Heaven (page 40), for example, requires a Run of 2 to 8, while Red Lantern (page 43) needs a Run of 1 to 7. These and other requirements are clearly marked on each of the photographed Hand Cards.

KONG – Any <u>Four identical tiles.</u> If you make a Kong, you then have to take one of the loose tiles from the wall, then discard one tile to end your turn.

FLOWERS – The flower tiles are not part of your hand except Heavenly Paradise, where a Bouquet is required (see Page 71). When picked up, a flower is placed, face up, in front of that players rack before taking a replacement from the loose tiles. These flowers are scored at the end of the round. See scoring (page 19)

Option: Keep all flowers hidden (face down). However, there is no benefit to the game by doing this, and a player mistaking a One of Bamboo for a flower may go unnoticed until the end of the game.

BOUQUET - There are eight flowers – Two sets numbered 1 to 4 – One with Red* and one with Black* numbers. A Bouquet is a <u>full set of 1 to 4</u> of the <u>same color</u>. (*See page 5 for set variations).

JOKERS – These (if supplied) should remain in the box. They <u>are not used</u> in traditional Mahjong and unbalance both the game and its scoring.

THE BASICS – START PLAYING

Now, this is where Griggy's Universal Mahjong rivals other guides: With the hands, all photographed with clearly displayed scores, Griggy's encourages you to clear the table and start playing! Unable to remember all those terms and elements? It doesn't matter - The Hands Cards remind you and make everything clear. Before long you should be calling, "MAH JONG!"

SETTING UP

You will need a reasonably big table to play Mahjong – preferably a square card table with sides between 32 and 50 inches (81-127cm).

First, you need to lay all the tiles face down (remove any Jokers or Spare tiles – these are not going to be needed). The tiles are shuffled; this is known as 'the Twittering of the Sparrows' or 'Washing the tiles.' All players take turns to push the tiles around the table to mix them up.

Next, you need to build the wall. In a four-player game, each player builds their side. Lay 18 tiles out in a straight line in front of you, then place another tile on top of each. Use your rack to both ensure the tiles are straight and assist pushing your wall together with the others. The wall to your right should join it from the inside (so it does not get any longer). The wall of the player to your left should join your wall on the outside so that it does make it longer.

There should be no tiles left over or any gaps once the wall is constructed correctly.

THE MAHJONG COMPASS

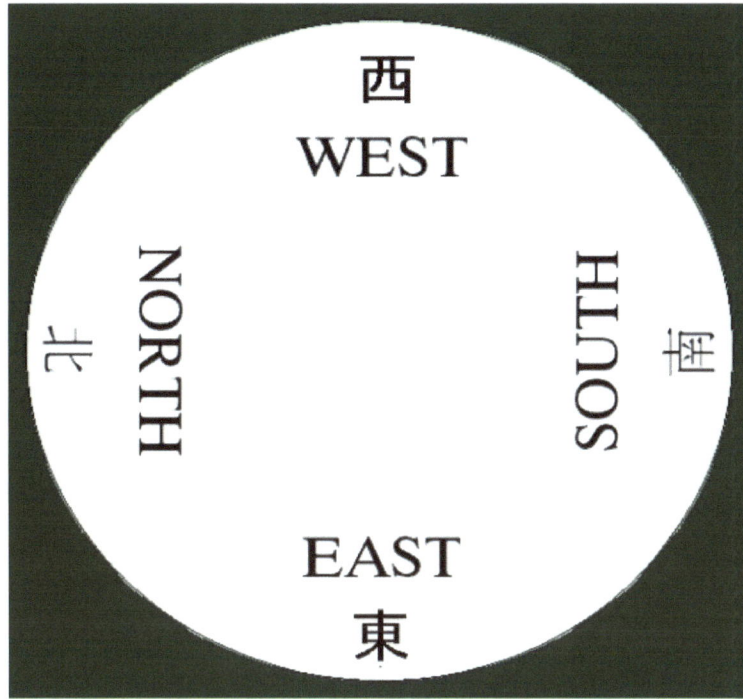

Once the wall is constructed, each player should throw the two dice. Whoever throws the highest number, becomes the East Wind Player (*EAST*).

The Mahjong compass is the reverse of a Northern Hemisphere one. So, the player to the right of East Wind is South; the player opposite is West and the player to East Wind's left is North.

Record, who starts as *EAST* and ensure they have the Marked Rack.

WIND OF THE ROUND

For the first round, the 'Wind-of-the-Round' is always EAST. The Wind-of-the-Round only changes when *EAST* next regains the East Wind title and the Marked Rack. So, for the wind to change, *EAST* must first lose the rack, then get it back again, usually by calling "Mah Jong!"

Mahjong sets include a set of large plaques – one for each of the winds of the rounds (or prevailing winds as they were once called). Place the Plaque (or card) that is marked East Wind, face up on the table. That is the Wind-of-the-Round.

The Wind-of-the-Round is rarely needed until a player completes a hand by calling "Mah Jong!" or the wall runs out of tiles. See Scoring (page 19).

A trick you can use to keep the Wind-of-the-Round tiles in order is to stack them in advance. When the original East Wind player becomes East again, take the top plaque and put it on the bottom of the pile. Stack them in this order (top down) EAST, SOUTH, WEST, NORTH. (The Chinese Mahjong compass is read anti-clockwise – the same as the order of play in Mahjong).

BREAKING THE WALL

Now, you are almost ready to start playing the first round. All the players need to get their initial tiles; This distribution is the East Wind player's (*EAST's*) responsibility.

EAST rolls the dice again. Starting from their wall, *EAST* counts anti-clockwise around the sides of the wall until they reach the number thrown. (So, if *EAST* throws a 5, they would end up back at their own wall). Then, *EAST* counts the same number of tiles, from the left end of that wall. Where *EAST* ends up is where the wall is broken. *EAST* takes a stack of two tiles from this position and places them, still face down, on the wall at clockwise (left) end. These two tiles are the Loose Tiles on the wall.

DISTRIBUTING THE TILES – TRADITIONAL METHOD

EAST breaks the wall further, by removing a chunk of four tiles to the right of this new gap. Each player then takes their turn in an anti-clockwise direction from *EAST*, to take four tiles from the same (right hand) end of the wall. Continue to do this until all players have twelve tiles (North, the player to *EAST's* left, will be the last player to pick up their four tiles). Then, *EAST* takes the next top row tile, skips the next and takes the one beyond it. *EAST*, now has fourteen tiles. The remaining players each take one tile from the same end, leaving them with thirteen tiles each.

If any player gets a flower or flowers, as tiles a dealt out, then they should display the flower (or flowers), face up in front of their rack. Take Loose Tiles to replace these tiles in your rack and replace the loose tiles with those from the same end. It is possible that a loose tile is also a flower if so, display this flower too and take another loose tile.

PREFERRED OPTION FOR DISTRIBUTING THE TILES

It is common that, during the distribution of the tiles, impatient players may take tiles out of order and that those swapping flowers for loose tiles may miss their turn to pick up. One successful method to prevent this is to promote *EAST* to *Dealer*. *EAST* then hands out all the tiles, just as described above. However, no flowers can be exchanged until all tiles have dealt out. Players then exchange any flowers with the loose tiles, in anti-clockwise order from *EAST*.

Other instructions include complex rules for the player order in which flowers are replaced by Loose Tiles depending upon the player's wind and the wind of the round. However, as the tiles were all shuffled, it makes no difference at this stage of the game, and I have chosen not to describe these overly complex options.

It should also be noted that there are many variations of how the wall is broken and the initial tiles distributed. If you are a veteran player and prefer a different method, then feel free to continue as you were. As long as *East* ends up with fourteen tiles and the other players thirteen, then it doesn't matter.

Before play starts, each player can take some time to sort their tiles and decide what hand/s they may wish to try to complete by comparing the tiles they have with to those photographed in the Hand Cards section. Notice that there are hands based on certain suits or Honour tiles and that these have been grouped together where possible.

HELP CHOOSING A HAND

Your rack has many tiles from the same suit. Consider Purity Suit Hand (Page 25) or All Pair Hand (Page 33).

You have a lot of two different suits then have a look at Gertie's Garden (page 44) or Mixed Pung Hand (page 45)

You appear to have a random hand with no or few matching tiles. Look for matching numbers for either Knitting Pairs (page 31) or Tripple Knitting (page 32), if you also have some Winds, maybe try Windy Chows (page 35).

Lots of Suit tiles from all three Suits? – Then, again, Mixed Pung Hand (page 45).

Do you have the makings of a Run and some Winds and/or Dragons? Gretta's Garden (page 57) may be a good choice.

There are also sections based on having a lot of any of the following:

Bamboo (page 61), Circles (page 50), Characters (page 46), Wind and Dragon (page 54)

Starting with Pungs from differing suits that are One's or Nines with Dragons and Winds should lead you to the All Honours hand (page 26)

If you think you may have been dealt a complete hand, first check it then see the Hands of Good Fortune (page 70).

PLAY STARTS:

EAST has to discard the first tile to begin the game. Discarded tiles (discards) are placed, face up, in the middle of the walls. As they are discarded, the player putting them down should announce what tile they are discarding. Option: In the original Chinese game, all discards were laid face down requiring players to remember all those discarded. I do not recommend this option for American Mahjong unless all players have exceptional memories.

Play now continues in an anti-clockwise direction, with players either drawing the next wall tile (clockwise from where the wall was broken) or choosing to take and create an exposed (unconcealed) element using the tile the previous player discarded.

Important: Any player wishing to pick up a discard to create a Pung, Chow, Kong or Complete a hand, must do so before the next player discards. After this, it becomes a 'dead tile' and can not be picked up by any player. This is a good time to remember that there are only four of each tile.

Any player picking up a flower from the wall (flowers cannot be discarded), must display this flower in front of their rack and replace it with a tile from the Loose tiles BEFORE discarding a tile to end their turn.

Not all elements can be exposed and allow a player to pick up a discard. Only creating Pungs (three of the same tile), Kongs (four of the same tile) or Chows (three tiles with consecutive numbers in the same suit) allow you to pick up the tile just discarded. The discard that you pick up must be used and displayed in your element (Pung, Kong or Chow). These tiles are now exposed and therefore can't be used to complete a concealed hand or benefit from a Buried Treasure bonus. It is usual practice to announce what element you have made when claiming a discard. End your turn by discarding a tile from your rack. You can never discard a tile from an exposed element.

Any player can claim a discarded tile to form an exposed Pung, Chow or Kong. Once they do this, play continues in an anti-clockwise direction from that player. This does mean that players can miss their turn. This is a feature of the game and the reason hands that are Concealed or Semi-Concealed hand reward players with a higher score than similar hands that allow discards.

Forming a Kong (Four of a Kind), by picking up a discard.

If you already have a Pung (three of a kind), concealed in your rack, and you wish to pick up the forth, you must expose the Kong (face up in front of your rack **and** then pick up another tile from the loose tiles, on the wall.

If you have an exposed Pung and a player discards the fourth (final tile) – you can NOT pick up the discard to make a Kong.

Forming a Kong (Four of a Kind), by picking up a tile from the wall.

If adding the fourth tile to a concealed Pung in your rack, creates a Kong, you must declare it, lay it out in front of your rack and pick another tile from the loose tiles. This still counts as a concealed Kong. Players often leave one or two of the tiles face down to indicate this. However, you do not have to create a Kong – If you wish you can discard the final tile and leave the concealed Pung in your rack.

Important: You can not pick up a discarded tile to form any of the following elements unless you complete a hand by doing so and, only then if the hand is not fully concealed: PAIR, any RUN or KNITTING.

Each player, unless declaring "Mah Jong!", ends their turn by discarding a tile.

It is always wise to check you have the right number of tiles in your possession – that's those concealed in your rack plus any exposed. Before you play and after your turn, you should have thirteen tiles (count any Kongs as if they only have three tiles each). The only exception is when you create a Mah Jong, where no tile is discarded – All Mah Jong's have fourteen tiles (Counting Kongs as having three tiles).

That's the basics covered. You are playing Mahjong! – Play continues until one of two things happen. Either someone completes a hand and calls "Mah Jong!" or, alternatively, you use up all the tiles on the wall.

Remember – If you need only one tile to complete a hand, you are Fishing. You should clearly state to all other players when this happens. Knowing a player is close to completing a hand may encourage them to try to go for an easier hand to beat you to the call.

Honours.

Mahjong values the Winds, Dragons, One's and Nines as special. All of these are known as Honours. Many of the higher scoring hands use these, so, when sorting your rack, don't be too quick to discard them. However, this previously rather complex part of the game has been completely replaced - printed on the Hand Cards is both the full score and the score for fishing. The formula remains complicated, but the hard work has all been done for you.

Flowers.

Any player who picks up a flower from the wall displays it for all to see in front of their rack. They then pick another tile from the loose tiles on the wall. flowers are counted at the end of the round. They are not part of any Hand, but a Bouquet of flowers (all four of the same color) is required to complete the Heavenly Paradice Hand. Flowers are scored at the end of the round see 'Scoring' on the next page.

Loose Tiles.

The two tiles on the far, anti-clockwise, end of the wall that are used to replace flower tiles and the extra tile used in Kongs are called Loose Tiles. As they are taken to replace flowers or after a Kong is made, the player nearest that end of the wall should replace them with tiles from the same end of the wall. The replacement, Loose Tiles must remain face down, they are just elevated to the third level of the wall – always at the far, anti-clockwise end of the wall.

If *EAST* was declared as 'dealer' (Distributing all the tiles at the start of the game), then *EAST* also replaces any loose tiles taken during play.

END OF THE ROUND – SCORING

Now, as described earlier, there are usually only two ways that a round can end: Either play stops because a player completes a hand and calls "Mah Jong!" Alternatively, the wall runs out of tiles before anyone completes a hand. Should this happen, a DEAD ROUND or GOULASH is declared. We are going to call it a *Goulash* because we like that name! It is also remotely possible that a round will end because a player completes the Heavenly Paradise Hand (Page 74). Completing this, rare hand, ends not just the round but the whole game!

MAH JONG IS CALLED

The player that calls "Mah Jong!" is the winner of the round. Play stops and the caller must lay out all their tiles and state which hand they have completed. The other players may check the relevant Hand Card to confirm that it is complete and complies with the hand's rules. The winner of the round will also the next round's *EAST* player taking the marked rack and starting the next round.

The winner of the round scores the value printed on the Hand Card, doubling that score if Buried Treasure is an option and the hand was concealed. They also receive points for flowers or bouquets of flowers they have collected (see next page for options to score the flowers.)

FISHING - SCORING

Any players who were Fishing (needing one tile to complete a hand) when "Mar Jong!" was called gets the Fishing score, printed on the Hand Card of the hand they were collecting. Fishing usually awards half the Mah Jong score but, there are some exceptions.

Any player holding a Pung of all three Dragons would score 1000 unless they completed the hand, The Three Great Scholars – page 60, which scores 1700 (in a four-player game)

FLOWERS – SIMPLIFIED SCORING

Four Player Game: All players get 100 for every single flower (not in a bouquet) and 1000 for each Bouquet. Two Player Game: All players get 50 for every single flower and 500 for a Bouquet.

FLOWERS-TRADITIONAL SCORING (OPTIONAL)

Here is an optional, and more complex, a method of scoring the flowers that replaces the simplified method described above. It is included because many veteran players prefer this. Feel free to try both and make your own choice.

The flower tiles are each marked with both a Wind and a number.

EAST — PLUMB   SOUTH — ORCHID   WEST — CHRYSANTHEMUM   NORTH — BAMBOO

A single flower scores 4 points, but this can be multiplied many times: A flower's score is doubled if is the Wind of the Round and doubled again if it is held by the player who is the same Wind. Do this with all flowers held and add the results together. If the flowers held, form a Bouquet then the result is doubled three more times (not multiplied by three!). Should a player be exceptionally lucky and hold all eight flowers (has two Bouquets) then the result is doubled three times again and would result in the maximum possible flower score of 3072. (4+4+4+4+8+8+8+8=48)x2x2x2x2x2x2).

Too complicated? – Scoring the flowers is always a 'more-luck-than-skill' part of the game and reverting to the Simplified Scoring method (see the previous page), does balance the game in favor of skill and can save you much time between rounds.

SCORING INCOMPLETE HANDS

The following scoring applies only to players who were neither fishing <u>nor</u> completed a hand when the round ended with another player calling "Mah Jong!" These players receive, as well as the flowers score (by whichever method you choose) the following fixed amounts for completing some of the Elements that they may have collected.

Regardless of the hand, they were trying to collect; if they required more than one tile to complete the hand (were not fishing), they should receive points for the following elements.

Pungs = 5 each. – Honours Pungs=10 each – Either doubled if concealed.

Kongs = 10 each. -Honours Kongs 20 each – Either doubled if concealed.

Chows, Pairs, Knitting, and Runs do not score anything at all.

That's it! – Scoring sorted. Record the scores, and you're ready to shuffle the tiles and start the next round.

Remember to ensure that the Marked Rack gets passed to the player who called "Mah Jong!" – They are the new *EAST*. If nobody completed a hand, then see the next page Goulash.

See page 22 for how to end the whole game.

GOULASH

So, the wall ran out of tiles, and nobody completed a hand – What do you score? – NOTHING! – No player scores anything at all. You don't even get anything for a Bouquet. *EAST* loses their title and the marked rack to the player opposite who becomes *EAST*.

The tiles are all returned to the table and shuffled again. You then build your walls with *EAST* breaking the wall and dealing out the tiles as exactly as described previously. Remember: *EAST* starts with fourteen tiles and the other players all start with thirteen.

In a Goulash round, everyone has a greater chance to complete a hand because all players can exchange, up to nine, unwanted tiles with the other players before the round starts.

First, each player picks three unwanted tiles from their rack and exchanges them (keeping them hidden) with the player opposite. Then each player picks another three and swaps them with the player on their left. Finally, each player selects three tiles and swaps them with the player to their right. You permitted to exchange tiles that another player just gave you.

Here's where Griggy's New Universal Mahjong differs from other, more complicated, instructions:

EAST starts the game by discarding their fourteenth tile, and the game then proceeds exactly as before.

Whoever is recording the scores, should note that the previous round resulted in a Goulash. If you have chosen to play a fixed number of rounds (see options to end the game on page 22), then the round that resulted in a Goulash does not count towards this number.

ENDING THE GAME

There are five different ways to end a game of Mahjong. You should decide which you are going to use before you complete the first round.

1: COMPLETE THE HEAVENLY PARADISE HAND

This is not optional and overrides all the following options to end the game.

The Heavenly Paradise hand (page 71) ends the whole game and wins it for the successful (and very lucky) player. This is regardless of the number of rounds that have been played or the current scores. However, there is little need to worry about having a very short game – Heavenly Paradise is an exceptionally rare hand.

2: PLAY A LIMITED NUMBER OF ROUNDS

Simply determine, in advance, how many rounds should be played before the game ends. Because Mahjong includes an element of luck, we recommend that at least eight hands should be played before declaring the game over.

New players may find that rounds can take up to half an hour to play, so a low number of rounds (such as eight) may be advisable. The most commonly accepted number of rounds is sixteen. Goulash's do not count as rounds.

3: PLAY UNTIL A SET SCORE IS REACHED

The first player to score X wins the game. A score of 15,000 is a popular choice because it is often achieved between fourteen and eighteen rounds.

If beginners are playing, you may wish to set a lower limit to make the game is shorter. It is accepted that those new to the game may take a while to learn to play at a faster rate.

4: ORIGINAL EAST CALLS EIGHT MAH JONGS

Play until the original East Wind Player wins or retains the Marked Rack back eight times. In other words, when *EAST* calls Mah Jong eight times.

We are no great fans of this option; it biases the first player to be *EAST* and often results in exceptionally long games

5: FOUR PREVAILING WINDS

Play continues until all four Wind-of-the-Rounds have been used. This would be when the East plaque or card comes back to the top of the pile. See Wind-of-the-Rounds (page 12). This can also benefit the first *EAST* player and, again, could result in very long games. However, this appears to be the most widely accepted method after playing sixteen rounds.

6: TIME LIMITED GAME

Useful if any player is only available for a certain time or another event will interrupt play. Set a fixed time in advance of play and tally the scores at this point. You may wish to finish the round in play. However, a game can be restarted another day. Simply finish a round, record the scores and finish the game another day.

Whichever method you choose, it is important that you establish this before play starts.

Griggy's New

1

Ordinary Suit Hand

UNIVERSAL

MAH JONG 1000*

Fishing 500

2-Player 500*

2-Player Fishing 250

*Buried Treasure! Call MAH JONG CONCEALED to Double your Score

This hand is 4x Pungs and a Pair from the same Suit. To make it easier, any can be substituted with Winds or Dragons.

If you don't need to use Dragons or Winds, you will score more because that would be a Purity Suit Hand (2)

Ordinary Suit Hand

ORDINARY SUIT HAND

Though the most basic hand that doesn't score highly, it is wise not to dismiss it. Being easy to collect means you may be able to call "Mah Jong!" before your opponents.

This example uses Circles and includes a Chow (run of three) The Ordinary Suit Hand can also be made with all Bamboo or all Characters. The Chow is optional, replacing one of the Pungs.

Kongs are not permitted in this hand. Only one Chow is allowed in all hands except Windy Chows (page 35).

PURITY SUIT HAND

Griggy's New

2

Purity Suit Hand

UNIVERSAL

**MAH JONG
1400***

**Fishing
700**

2-Player 700*

**2 Player Fishing
350**

*Buried Treasure!
Call MAH JONG
CONCEALED to
Double your Score*

The Purity Suit Hand is similar to the Ordinary Suit Hand (1)
except that Dragons and Winds are not permitted.

It is 4x Pungs and a Pair all from the same suit
(All Circles, Bamboo or Characters)

Kongs are not allowed unless you are attempting
to complete Plucking the Plumb Blossom (26) in
which case Buried Treasure does not apply.

Purity Suit Hand

The Purity Suit Hand is one of the most popular being both easy to remember and offering a reasonable score.

 It is made with tiles all from the same suit. This example uses Circles, but it can also be constructed with all Bamboo or all Characters.

This is the first hand to offer the Buried Treasure incentive – Make this hand from wall tiles only (concealed), to double the Mah Jong score. This does not affect fishing scores.

ALL HONOURS HAND

Griggy's New

3

All Honours

UNIVERSAL

MAH JONG 1800 *

Fishing 900

2-Player 900 *

2-Player Fishing 450

All Honours or 1's & 9's is another 4x Pungs and a Pair hand. This time the Suits can be mixed but all must be Honours tiles. Honours are: 1's, 9's, Dragons and Winds.

Kongs are not permitted.

*Buried Treasure! Call MAH JONG CONCEALED to Double your Score

All Honours Hand

Another four Pungs and a Pair hand, All Honours is one of only a few hands that permits a mix of different suits. That alone would make the hand incredibly simple to make but, as the title suggests, it's never going to be quite that easy! All the elements must be made from Honours: Winds, Dragons, Ones, and Nines. Any combination of the Honours can be used.

Bear in mind that collecting Honours tiles may deny your opponents from completing many of the higher scoring hands.

ALL KONG HAND

Griggy's New

4

All Kong Hand

UNIVERSAL

MAH JONG
2000

Fishing
1000

2-Player 500

2-Player Fishing
250

All Kong Hand

One of the hardest hands to complete, All Kong Hand
requires 4x Kongs and a Pair from the same Suit.
Any of the Kongs or the Pair can be substituted with
Dragons and/or Winds.

The All Kong Hand appears to be a quick way to grab a high score. However, Kongs are difficult to collect because you need all four matching tiles. Any opponent collecting runs, a chow or pairs from your chosen suit is likely to deny you the chance to collect all four. The All Kong Hand requires you to collect four Kongs and all from the same suit. Dragons and Winds can be used to substitute any of the Kongs or the Pair.

Remember, when making Kongs, should declare them and pick up a Loose Tile after each one is completed.

WRIGGLY SNAKE

Wriggly Snake

Griggy's New

5

Wriggly Snake

UNIVERSAL

MAH JONG
1400

Fishing
700

2-Player 700

2 Player Fishing
350

SEMI-CONCEALED HAND

This hand requires a full run (1 to 9) of any of the three Suits together with one of each Wind with an extra of any to make a Pair.

This is a Semi-Concealed Hand - Only the last tile can be a Discard.

Wriggly Snake is the first hand to employ a Run, this one being a full run of One to Nine. Runs are easy to collect in one respect and difficult in another: It is likely that your opponents are collecting the most popular element – the Pung, leaving one of each tile available for you to collect. However, you can't pick up discards to make a Run; all must come from the wall except the last tile - Wriggly Snake is semi-concealed.

Look at your opponents exposed Pungs as well as the discards. Abandon your run if all four of any appear on the table unless you are fishing (needing only one tile to complete the hand), allowing you to collect the fishing score.

DRAGONFLY

Griggy's New

6

Dragonfly

UNIVERSAL

MAH JONG
1100

Fishing
550

2-Player 550

2-Player Fishing
275

SEMI-CONCEALED HAND

Dragonfly

Dragonfly requires one of each of the three Dragons with a Pung of each of the three Suits (Circle, Bamboo and Character). Complete this hand with a Pair of any of the Suits.

This is a Semi-Concealed Hand - Only the last tile can be a Discard.

Dragonflies are one of the World's most colorful insects, and this is reflected in the Dragonfly hand. One of each color Dragon and a Pung from each of the three Suits recreate this wonderful creature.

Though a semi-concealed hand, Dragonfly is quite easy to collect and a popular choice if you find yourself with a very mixed suit hand. Just be aware that Dragonflies do not like windy conditions and that no Winds can be included.

CHINESE ODDS

Griggy's New

7

Chinese Odds

UNIVERSAL

MAH JONG
1800

Fishing
900

2-Player
900

2-Player Fishing
450

Chinese Odds

Chinese Odds is 4x Pungs, or Kongs and a Pair from the same Suit.
What makes it harder, is that all the numbers must be Odd.
This example uses Characters. You could also use
all Circles or all Bamboo.

Chinese Odds looks very much like a Purity Suit Hand, and indeed it is a Purity Suit Hand – All tiles must be from the same suit with Dragons and Winds excluded. It scores higher because all the tiles must be Odd Numbers.

It is not possible to create a 'Chinese Evens' hand simply because there are only four sets of even Numbers: (2,4,6 and 8). There is one hand that does demand even numbers, that is The Round Table (Page 53).

KNITTING PAIRS

SEMI-CONCEALED HAND

Knitting Pairs

Knitting Pairs id 7x Pairs of numbers all using the same two Suits. Each Pair must have one from each of the two Suits that you have chosen. No Pairs can include the third Suit. In this example Characters are the third (unused) Suit.

This is a Semi-Concealed Hand - Only the last tile can be a Discard.

Knitting in Mahjong refers to matching Numbers rather than Suits. It is employed in Knitting Pairs and again in Tripple Knitting (next page).

One of the easiest hands to complete because only one of each tile is required. You have a choice of any two of the three suits and have no restriction on which numbers you can use. You can even repeat pairs as in the example above.

TRIPPLE KNITTING

Griggy's New

9

Tripple Knitting

UNIVERSAL

MAH JONG
1000

Fishing
500

2-Player
500

2-Player Fishing
250

SEMI-
CONCEALED
HAND

Tripple Knitting

Tripple Knitting requires 4x sets of three tiles, each with matching numbers and each containing all three Suits. The hand is completed with a Pair of numbers using any two of the three Suits.

This is a Semi-Concealed Hand - Only the last tile can be a Discard.

Another very easy hand to construct, Tripple Knitting varies from Knitting Pairs (page 31) only in that it requires matching numbers from all three suits (with any two in the Pair).

It is easy to overlook Knitting when first looking at your rack of tiles. If you don't see many (or any) matching Suits or Honours then tiles, look out for matching numbers instead.

ALL PAIR HAND

SEMI-CONCEALED HAND

All Pair Hand

The All Pair Hand is simply 7x Pairs of the same number all from the same Suit. You may have 2x Pairs of the same number, but this does not form a Kong and no extra tile is picked up

This is a Semi-Concealed Hand - Only the last tile can be a Discard.

When collecting for the All Pair Hand, it often develops into a Purity Suit Hand. Though both hands score the same, the ability to pick up discarded tiles in the Purity Suit Hand often tempts the collector of the All Pair Hand to abandon it in favor of the Purity Suit Hand.

ALL PAIR HONOURS

Griggy's New

11

All Pair **HONOURS**

UNIVERSAL

MAH JONG
1800

Fishing
900

2-Player 900

2-Player Fishing
450

SEMI-CONCEALED HAND

All Pair Honours

This hand requires 7x Pairs of Honours tiles.
Honours are: 1's, 9's, Winds and Dragons.

This is a Semi-Concealed Hand - Only the last tile can be a Discard.

All Pair Honours is another hand that can easily morph into another. If collecting just Pairs of Honours tiles, you are unable to pick up discards. Therefore, it is tempting to pick up discards, make Pungs and convert this hand into an All Honours Hand. Both hands score the same, so there is no penalty if you abandon the All Pair Honours in favor of the All Honours Hand.

WINDY CHOWS

Griggy's New

12

Windy Chows

UNIVERSAL

MAH JONG
1000

Fishing
500

2-Player
500

2-Player Fishing
250

Windy Chows

This hand requires a Chow from each of the three Suits.
A Chow is a run of three - 2-3-4 , 7-8-9 etc.
The hand is completed with one of each Wind
plus one extra of any Wind to form a Pair.

Windy Chows may be your only option if you find yourself looking at a rack with few, or no, matching pairs or numbers. Collecting Chows (runs of three) is usually easy because the run can be any three consecutive numbers. Collect one of these in each of the three Suits, collecting the Winds as you go.

You can pick up discards to form Chows, but as soon as you expose more than one Chow, then your opponents will know you are going for Windy Chows – It is the only hand that allows more than one Chow!

HEAVENLY TWINS

Griggy's New

13

Heavenly Twins

UNIVERSAL

MAH JONG
1400

Fishing
700

2-Player 700

2 Player Fishing
350

SEMI-CONCEALED HAND

Heavenly Twins

Heavenly Twins requires 7x Pairs of matching numbers all from the same Suit. Any of the three Suits can be used.

This is a Semi-Concealed Hand - Only the last tile can be a Discard.

Find yourself with a lot of any one of the three suits; then you should consider trying to collect Heavenly Twins. You can't make Pairs by picking up discards so only the final tile can be a discard (it is a semi-concealed hand.)

Note: You require seven pairs from the nine available. So, keep a keen eye on the table – you won't be able to make a pair if three are already disclosed or have been discarded.

UNIQUE WONDER

Originally named 'The Thirteen Grades of Imperial Treasure,' Unique Wonder demands one of every Honours tile plus an extra of any of them.

Previously overvalued, probably due to the richness of its name, Griggy and I settled on a lower value based on the mathematical chances of obtaining it. Because your opponents are likely to be collecting Pungs, one of each tile often remain. However, you can't pick up any discards (except one to complete the hand), so it remains a moderately difficult hand.

WINDY ONES

Griggy's New

15

Windy Ones

UNIVERSAL

MAH JONG
1400*

Fishing
700

2-Player 700*

2 Player Fishing
350

SEMI-CONCEALED HAND

Windy Ones

This hand requires a Pung of 1's from each of the three Suits plus one of each of the four Winds with one extra of any Wind.

*Buried Treasure!
Call MAH JONG
CONCEALED to
Double your Score

This is a Semi-Concealed Hand - Only the last tile can be a Discard.

Windy Ones is a Buried Treasure Hand that can encourage the collector to gamble – Double or Fishing Score.

It is already Semi-Concealed, so it only allows the final tile to be a Discard. However, if you reject a discard and hold out for another from the wall, then you could double your score. Probably only wise to try this if you only need the second of any of the winds but it is up to you!

WINDY NINES

Griggy's New
16
Windy Nines
UNIVERSAL

MAH JONG
1400*

Fishing
700

2-Player 700*

2 Player Fishing
350

SEMI-CONCEALED HAND

Windy Nines

Windy Nines requires a Pung of 9's from each of the three Suits as well as one of each Wind and an extra of any wind to form a Pair.

This is a Semi-Concealed Hand - Only the last tile can be a Discard.

*Buried Treasure!
Call MAH JONG
CONCEALED to
Double your Score*

Windy Nines is easier to collect than you may first think because Nine's are less often used in Runs: Other hands include runs of One to Seven or Two to Eight. It is also less slightly less likely that a Chow will contain either a One or a Nine

Like Windy Ones, this hand encourages you to gamble with its Buried Treasure option. Would you risk sacrificing the Mah Jong Score for a chance to double it?

GATES OF HEAVEN

Griggy's New

17

Gates of Heaven

UNIVERSAL

MAH JONG
1800

Fishing
900

2-Player 900

2-Player Fishing
450

SEMI-CONCEALED HAND

Gates of Heaven

Using tiles from only one of the three Suits, construct a Pung of 1's, a Pung of 9's and a Run of 2 to 8. This example uses Characters but you could use all Bamboo or all Circles instead.

This is a Semi-Concealed Hand - Only the last tile can be a Discard.

Gates of Heaven is a tricky hand to complete because, like the Purity Suit Hand (page 25), it requires all fourteen tiles to be from the same Suit. It is also Semi-Concealed so the Pungs of Ones and Nines can't be made from discards unless you are fishing for that final tile.

A RUN, A PUNG AND A PAIR

Griggy's New

18

**A Run,
a Pung &
a Pair**

UNIVERSAL

MAH JONG
1500

Fishing
750

2-Player 750

2-Player Fishing
375

SEMI-CONCEALED HAND

A Run, a Pung and a Pair

Using tiles from only one Suit, build a full Run of 1 to 9, a Pung and a Pair. This is harder than it first appears because you will require all four of your Pung tiles and three of your Pair tiles.

This is a Semi-Concealed Hand - Only the last tile can be a Discard.

At first glance, this hand may appear to match Gates of Heaven (page 40), yet it doesn't score so well. This is because, although both hands contain a Run, here we have a complete Run of one to nine, with the choice to make the Pung and Pair from tiles of any number (from within the same Suit).

HEADS AND TAILS

Heads and Tails

Heads and Tails is an all 1's and 9's hand that requires 4x Pungs and a Pair made from any of the Suits. However, Kongs, Dragons and Winds are not permitted.

Heads and Tails is a 'Four Pungs and a Pair' hand requiring that all the elements are made from Ones and Nines.

It isn't a concealed hand so you can build the Pungs using discards. However, if you fancy a challenge and the chance to double your score, then try to collect this hand from wall tiles only.

RED LANTERN

Griggy's New

20

Red Lantern

UNIVERSAL

MAH JONG
1100*

Fishing
550

2-Player
550

2-Player Fishing
275

SEMI-CONCEALED HAND

Red Lantern

Red Lantern requires a Run of 1 to 7 in any Suit, with an extra of any in the Run to form a Pair. Complete the hand with a Pung of Red Dragons and a Pung of your Wind.

*Buried Treasure! Call MAH JONG CONCEALED to Double your Score

This is a Semi-Concealed Hand - Only the last tile can be a Discard.

Red Lantern is a good hand to aim for if you find yourself with Red Dragons and some of your Winds. It is another Semi-Concealed hand that tempts you to go fully concealed with the Buried Treasure option.

If you are unsure what Wind you are – look for the East Wind player (Their rack is the marked one, and they started the game) Then you can work it out from the Mahjong Compass on page 11.

GERTIE'S GARDEN

Griggy's New

21

Gertie's Garden

UNIVERSAL

MAH JONG
1400

Fishing
700

2-Player 700

2 Player Fishing
350

SEMI-CONCEALED HAND

Gertie's Garden

Gertie's Garden contains two Runs of 1 to 7
These can be made from any two of the three Suits.

This is a Semi-Concealed Hand - Only the last tile can be a Discard.

Gertie's Garden is an easy hand to remember and is, therefore, a very popular choice with it also providing a reasonable score.

You can't pick up discards to make Runs unless it is the final tile, so this is a Semi-Concealed hand.

MIXED PUNG HAND

Griggy's New

22

Mixed Pung Hand

UNIVERSAL

MAH JONG
1200

Fishing
600

2-Player 600

2-Player Fishing
300

FULLY CONCEALED HAND

Mixed Pung hand

The Mixed Pung Hand is 4x Pungs and a Pair made from any of the three Suits. These can be substituted by Winds or Dragons. To qualify as a Mixed Pung hand, it must include at least two Suits.

FULLY CONCEALED HAND - ALL TILES MUST COME FROM THE WALL

Not high-scoring, the Mixed Pung Hand is useful if you find a mixture of the three suits in your hand. However, bear in mind that this is a Fully Concealed hand – No tiles can be discards, including the last one.

THE CHARACTER HANDS

Many hands *can* use Characters, yet there are only three hands that dictate that Characters must be used. These hands, Lost Souls, Odd Characters and Red Arrow are together in this small section and is the first place to come if you get dealt a rack of mostly Character tiles.

Like the other suits, circles and Bamboo, they are numbered one to nine, and there are four of each of them in the set.

History of the Character tiles:

From the latest to the original Chinese Mahjong sets, the Character tiles are all marked with the same symbol, the *wàn* (萬) This means ten-thousand, but it also denotes wealth.

Along with the *wàn,* the tiles are numbered one to nine in Chinese. The set we have used also has the numbers printed in English but, if not, you will need to learn Chinese for one to nine! The numbers One, Two and Three are easy, and I hope that the picture (above) should help with the rest.

Character Hand

Lost Souls

Griggy's New

23

Lost Souls

UNIVERSAL

MAH JONG
2200

Fishing
1100

2-Player 1100

2 Player Fishing
550

SEMI-CONCEALED HAND

Lost Souls is a difficult hand to build - It requires 2x Pungs of Even Numbered Characters and a Pair of each of the four Winds.

This is a Semi-Concealed Hand - Only the last tile can be a Discard.

LOST SOULS

The first of only three Character hands, Lost Souls depicts two groups of even-numbered Pungs confused by the biddings of the Four Winds.

Harder to collect than you may first think because there are only four even-numbered Characters to choose from and should any of your opponents complete a Pung of Winds, they will thwart your efforts.

Character Hand

FULLY CONCEALED HAND

Odd Characters

The Odd Characters are 4x Pungs and a Pair of all Odd Numbered Characters

This hand differs from Chinese Odds (7) because only Characters can be used and it is Fully Concealed - No discards can be taken to make this hand.

ODD CHARACTERS

Odd Characters are often demanding, and these are no exception. The characters must be all odd numbers, and with four Pungs and a Pair, you need all of them (Numbers One, Three, Five, Seven and Nine). To make things even more difficult, you can't use any discards – this is a Fully Concealed Hand.

However, success is well rewarded, Odd Character's Mah Jong score is only exceeded by three, near impossible hands! See Hands of Good Fortune (page 70).

Character Hand

Griggy's New

25

Red Arrow

UNIVERSAL

MAH JONG
1500*

Fishing
750

2-Player 750*

2-Player Fishing
375

Red Arrow's shaft is 5x Pairs of Characters and its
tip is made with 2x Pairs of Red Dragons.
Note: The two Pairs of Dragons have not formed a Kong.

Red Arrow

***Buried Treasure!**
Call MAH JONG
CONCEALED to
Double your Score

RED ARROW

It is well worth trying to for Red Arrow should you find yourself with Pairs of Characters or Red Dragons.

Do not be tempted to convert the Dragons into a Kong because you cannot split them up again and doing so would leave you with one tile too many to make the pairs.

THE CIRCLE HANDS

Like the Characters, Circles only have three hands dedicated to them. However, do not dismiss the Circles, these three hands include two of the highest scoring, only beaten by Heavenly Paradise (page 71) which doesn't have a score!

As with the other two Suits, Circles are numbered from one to nine, and there are four of each of them, Like Bamboo, they usually have different colors (some sets two, and in our example set, three) but, unlike Bamboo, these colors are not specified within hands in most forms of the game.

When the game left China, many different names were added by different groups of players that only serve to confuse. Examples are Dots, Wheels, Cookies and even Oreo's (a modern American biscuit!). We are going to leave them as Circles because that's what they look like, but you are free to call them whatever you like.

History of the Circle tiles

Circles derived from the original Chinese game, where they were called Stones. These stones were depicted as flat river pebbles. Later the round shape was given the symbol 'tóng' (筒) which was a coin with a square hole in the middle.

Circle Hand

Plucking the Plumb Blossom from the Roof

This is a Purity Circles hand - All Circles 4x Pungs and a Pair - Kongs allowed.
*But it's not that simple... The final tile MUST be the 5 of Circles AND it must be drawn from the loose tiles on the wall.

Loose tiles can only be drawn after you either pick up a Flower or make a Kong. You can try to make Kongs from the other Pungs to increase your chances but that last tile must be the 5 of Circles. If this hand is completed another way, it scores as a Purity hand.

PLUCKING THE PLUMB BLOSSOM FROM THE ROOF

The hand with the longest name also scores joint highest because of its difficulty. Not only do you have to collect a Purity Hand of Circles, but you must complete the hand with the Five of Circles that must be drawn from the loose tiles on the wall (The Blossom on the Roof).

Not a Concealed hand, so try collecting it as purity Circles hand. Use discards to create Pungs (not the Fives) For the final Five, you either need to pick up a flower or pick up discards to convert your Pungs into Kongs, which also gives you a loose tile.

Circles Hand

Griggy's New

27

Plucking the Moon from the Sea Bed

UNIVERSAL

MAH JONG
3000

Fishing
700

2-Player 1500

2-Player Fishing
350

Plucking the Moon from the Sea Bed

Plucking the Moon is a Purity Circles Hand that allows Kongs.
But it is not that easy... The last tile must be from the wall,
it must be 1 of Circles AND it must be the very last tile on the wall!
Complete this hand any other way and it scores as a Purity Hand.

PLUCKING THE MOON FROM THE SEA BED

Joint highest score along with Plucking the Blossom from the Roof, Plucking the Moon (the One of Circles) from the Sea Bed relies on both skill and more than a little good luck.

You can't know what the last tile on the wall is going to be until there is only one left. Even then, you only stand a one-in-four chance of being the player who gets it.

I advise building this as a Circles Purity Suit Hand and hope the last tile is the One of Circles. However, it is more likely that it will appear among the discards or another player has it in their rack.

Circle Hand

Griggy's New

28

The Round Table

UNIVERSAL

MAH JONG
1800

Fishing
900

2-Player 900

2-Player Fishing
450

The Round Table

The Round Table consists of 4 Pungs or Kongs of even number Circles with a Pair of Red Dragons.

THE ROUND TABLE

The easiest of the Circle Hands, The Round Table is the hand to go for should you have a rack with six or more, even numbered Circle tiles.

Kongs are permitted but do not improve your score unless you fail to get as far as a fishing hand. See Scoring incomplete hands (Page 20).

This section includes hands that require Dragons and Winds to complete them.

Note: These are not all the hands that require Winds and Dragons but are those that require at least seven Winds and Dragons. There is an overlap with some of the Bamboo Hands, many of which also employ the services of the Winds and Dragons. These you will find in the Bamboo Hands section – page 61.

The Four Winds and the Three Dragons are all Honours tiles and are much respected and symbolic to the Chinese.

History of the Winds

Winds have always featured the four principal compass directions: 西 (*xī*) -West, 南 (*nán*) -South, 東 (*dōng*) –East and 北,(*běi*) -North.

Some Mahjong sets do not include the translation so you may need to either learn these symbols or otherwise mark the front of the tiles.

History of the Dragons

The Dragons or 'Arrows' represent virtues. Over time these have been interpreted into many meanings. However, there is a strong link to archery, the Chinese Imperial exam and also, although there are only three Dragons, they are associated with the five cardinal virtues of Confucius:

The White (*bái*) Dragon may mean either a miss in archery, one who has great respect for their elders and ancestors or one who is incorruptible.

The Green (*fā - wealth*) Dragon represents either the release of an arrow or the virtue of (*Li*) propriety and sincerity.

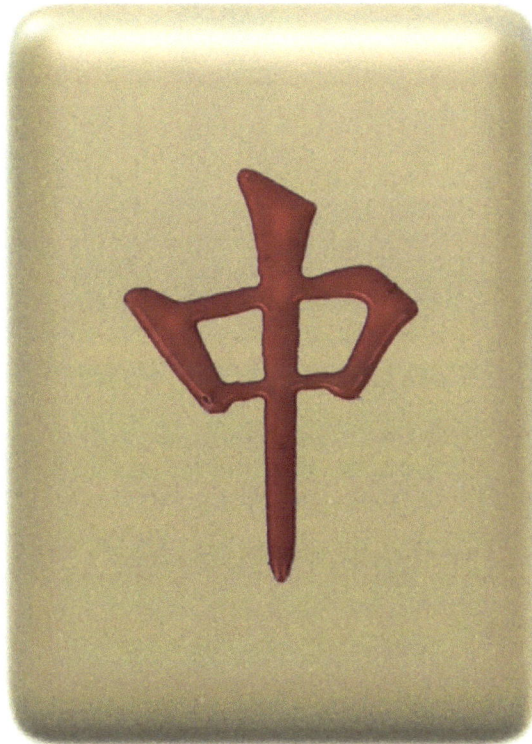

Finally, the Red Dragon (中)- zhōng is the hardest to directly translate having many meanings, including 'among,' 'center', 'within' and 'hit the mark.' However, these can all be associated with accuracy in archery. Also linked with the virtue of (*Ren*) meaning benevolence as well as passing the Imperial exam.

Whatever meanings you choose to apply to the Dragons, they remain the most popular suit with all of them required in the ultimate, game-winning hand: Heavenly Paradise – page 71.

Wind & Dragon Hand

All Wind and Dragon

All Wind and Dragon is just that - 4x Pairs and a Pung using only Dragons and Winds. This hand must include both Winds and Dragons

ALL WIND AND DRAGON

With the popularity of all Suit hands such as Purity Suit Hand and Gertie's Garden, there could be an abundance of these honour tiles up for grabs. Though it is possible to build this hand using all Winds, don't - Dragons must be included!

Kongs are permitted, and this is not a Concealed Hand, so you are free to pick up discards to make either Pungs or Kongs of your Dragons and Winds. Remember, you can't pick up discards to make the Pair unless it is the final tile.

Wind & Dragon Hand

SEMI-CONCEALED HAND

Gretta's Garden

*In Gretta's Garden we find... A Run of 1 to 7,
one of each of the four Winds and
one of each of the three Dragons*

This is a Semi-Concealed Hand - Only the last tile can be a Discard.

GRETTA'S GARDEN

Not all Wind and Dragon hands score well, and this is an example that is very easy to collect.

Because you can't pick up discards to form runs or the sets of Winds and Dragons, this is a Semi-Concealed Hand – You can only pick up a discarded tile to complete the hand.

Wind & Dragon Hand

Griggy's New

31

Three Great Scholars

UNIVERSAL

MAH JONG
1700

Fishing
850

2-Player 850

2-player Fishing
425

THREE GREAT SCHOLARS

The Three Great Scholars are represented by a Pung of each of the three Dragons. So special are the these that any player holding all the Scholars will score 1000* even if they do not complete the hand. To complete the hand and obtain the full Mah Jong score, you must also collect a Pung or Chow and a Pair of any Suit.

*Holding the three Scholars scores 1000 in Four Player Game and 500 in a Two Player Game.

THE THREE GREAT SCHOLARS

The Pung and Pair, if Suits must be from the same suit. If using a Chow, the pair must also be of the same suit. Optionally, you may make the Pung *and* Pair from any of the Winds

In this hand, you can't mix Winds with Suits.

Collecting all three Pungs of the Dragons is worth 1000 points, and this applies to all incomplete or fishing hands unless a Goulash is declared.

Wind & Dragon Hand

Griggy's New

32

Windy Dragons

UNIVERSAL

MAH JONG
1800

Fishing
900

2-Player 900

2-Player Fishing
450

Windy Dragons

Windy Dragons is 2x Pungs or Kongs of Dragons. These can be any two of the tree Dragons. Complete the hand with a Pair of each of the four Winds.

WINDY DRAGONS

Windy Dragons are the second all Wind and Dragon hand and the one to aim for if you have a mix of more than two of the Winds along with some Dragons.

Not a Concealed Hand, so you may pick up discarded Dragons to complete the Pungs or Kongs. You can only take a discard to complete a Pair if it also completes the hand (i.e., you are Fishing.) otherwise the tiles for the Pair must be collected from the wall.

Wind & Dragon Hand

Griggy's New

33

The Four Blessings

UNIVERSAL

MAH JONG 2000

Fishing 1000

2-Player 1000

2Player Fishing 500

The Four Blessings

The Four Blessings are the four winds and to complete this hand, you need pungs or Kongs of all four of them. Complete the hand with a Pair of anything.

THE FOUR BLESSINGS

You got me! There aren't any Dragons in this hand. I wasn't going to make a new section just for this one hand. However, it certainly is a hand worth collecting with rich rewards for collecting Pungs or Kongs of all four Winds and that single Pair of anything. It is not demoted to All Wind and Dragon (page 56) if you make the Pair from Winds

The Four Blessings is not a Concealed Hand, so you are free to pick up discards to make the Pungs or Kongs.

THE BAMBOO HANDS

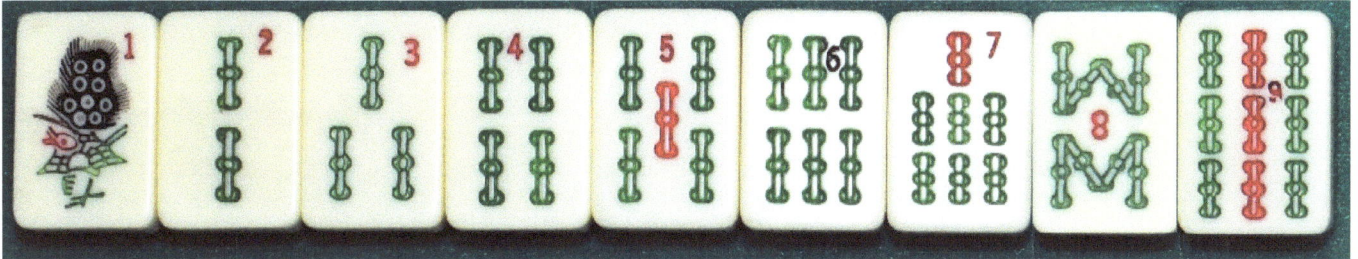

With eight Bamboo Hands, it is clear that Bamboo ranks above the other Suits, with Character and Circle hands each having only three dedicated hands. This being known, you would think that Bamboo hands would be harder to collect than either Circles or Characters. However, experienced Mahjong players soon balance this by choosing to collect Circles or Characters because they are likely to be more prolific.

Green Bamboo

Notice that some bamboo tiles are all green; those numbered 2,3,4,6 and 8 – These are the Green Bamboo.

Red Bamboo

The others have red parts, those numbered 1,5,7 and 9 and form the Red Bamboo. Please ignore that fact that my example set has a red eight printed on it – 8 is a Green Bamboo!

History of the Bamboo tiles.

Most players refer to this Suit as Bamboo, although some call them 'Sticks' or 'Poles' However, originally they were coins. Sets still retain a reference to this on their portrayal of the Bamboo. They were chains (*sǔo*) of copper coins that had a hole in the middle. The One of Bamboo is different, depicting a flower with a colorful bird. Some players refer to the One of Bamboo as 'the bird'.

Bamboo Hand

Griggy's New

34

Red Lily

UNIVERSAL

MAH JONG
1800

Fishing
900

2-Player 900

2-Player Fishing
450

Red Lily

Red Lily requires a Pung or Kong of both Red and White Dragons with 2x Pungs or Kongs of Red Bamboo and a Pair of Red Bamboo (1's, 5's, 7's and 9's are the Red Bamboo)

RED LILY

Red Lily is one of a few Bamboo hands that, though mostly Bamboo, could also qualify to go in the Dragons and Wind section.

It is also an example of a hand that specifies the color of the bamboo: Red Lily needs Red Bamboo, and there are fewer of these than there are of Green variety. It is this stipulation on Bamboo color that causes these hands to score more highly.

Red Lily is not a Concealed Hand so pick up discards to complete the Pungs or Kongs.

Bamboo Hand

Griggy's New
35
Ruby Jade
UNIVERSAL

MAH JONG
1800

Fishing
900

2-Player 900

2-Player Fishing
450

Ruby Jade Hand

Ruby Jade is a Pung or Kong of Red and Green Dragons with
a Pung or Kong of both Red and Green Bamboo
Complete the hand with any Pair of Bamboo

RUBY JADE HAND

Ruby Jade wants Red Dragons and Bamboo as well as their Green equivalents.

This is a hand to go for if your rack is a mix of Bamboo and Dragons. Discarding any White Dragons early on may fool your opponents into discarding the Dragons that you do want.

Not a Concealed Hand, Ruby Jade encourages you to complete those Pungs or Kongs with discards.

Bamboo Hand

SEMI-CONCEALED HAND

All Pair Ruby Jade

All Pair Ruby Jade requires a Pair of both Red and Green Dragons with 5x Pairs of Bamboo. The Pairs of Bamboo must include both Red and Green Bamboo.

This is a Semi-Concealed Hand - Only the last tile can be a Discard.

ALL PAIR RUBY JADE

Any All-Pair hand is going to have to be at least Semi-Concealed because of the Pairs. Though this is balanced when you consider that you only need to collect two of the four possible tiles.

Here, you need both Red and Green Dragons as well as Red and Green Bamboo's, but the mix is relatively easy to pick up.

Bamboo Hand

Griggy's New

37

Lily of the Valley

UNIVERSAL

MAH JONG
1800

Fishing
900

2-Player 900

2-Player Fishing
450

Lily of the Valley

Lily of the Valley requires a Pung or Kong of both White and Green Dragons accompanied by 2x Pungs or Kongs and a Pair of Green Bamboo.
The Green Bamboo are numbered 2,3,4,6 and 8

LILY OF THE VALLEY

All the Bamboo in this hand must be Green. No part of a Lily of the Valley is red, so only White and Green Dragons are included. Slightly easier to collect than Red Lily, yet we have scored it the same based on our scoring formula.

Lily of the Valley is one of Griggy's favorite hands, but see Sparrow Sanctuary (page 69) for an explanation as to why having favored hands can be a disadvantage.

Bamboo Hand

Royal Ruby

The Royal Ruby is a Red Bamboo hand requiring 3x Pungs or Kongs, plus a Pair, of Red Bamboo with a Pung or Kong of Red Dragons.

ROYAL RUBY

Royal Ruby is an All Red hand. A reminder: The Red Bamboo are numbered 1,5,7 and 9 (There are only four of them) so, unless you start with a rack heavy with Red Bamboo, this is not the Bamboo hand to choose. Instead, you might consider the, lower scoring but easier, All Pair Ruby Jade hand? (page 64)

Bamboo Hand

Imperial Jade

Imperial Jade is a 'all green' hand made with Green Bamboo and a Pung or Kong of Green Dragons. The Green Bamboo tiles are numbered 2,3,4,6 and 8. Using only these, from 3x Pungs (or Kongs) and a Pair. You can substitute one of the Pungs with a Chow if you need to.

IMPERIAL JADE

If your rack is looking decidedly green, then this has got to be the high-scoring hand to collect. It isn't a Concealed Hand, so pick up those Green Bamboo or Dragons as they appear to complete either Pungs or Kongs. Just remember, that unless you are fishing, you can't pick up discards to create the Pair.

Bamboo Hand

SEMI-CONCEALED HAND

All Pair Jade

The All Pair Jade hand demands only Green Bamboo and at least one Pair of Green Dragons. 7 Pairs in all are required and ALL must be green. You will notice that you will need to collect all four of at least one tile (in this example this is the 2's of Bamboo), but this does not form a Kong - they remain 2x Pairs and no extra tile is picked up as with a Kong.

ALL PAIR JADE

You may wonder why the All Pair Jade hand gives a score higher than the other similar hands such as All Pair Ruby Jade. The reason is that, to form seven pairs of Green Bamboo, you are required to collect all four of one of them. Our scoring formula regards this as a Kong although the hand does not – It regards them as two Pairs.

Bamboo Hand

Griggy's New

41

Sparrow Sanctuary

UNIVERSAL

MAH JONG
1900

Fishing
950

2-Player 950

2-Player Fishing
475

SEMI-CONCEALED HAND

Sparrow Sanctuary

In Sparrow Sanctuary, 2x Pairs of the 1 of Bamboo represent
the Sparrows. The remaining five Pairs must all
be made from Green Bamboo (Numbers 2,3,4,6 and 8)
The two Pairs of 1's of Bamboo do not form a Kong.

This is a Semi-Concealed Hand - Only the last tile can be a Discard.

SPARROW SANCTUARY

Sparrow Sanctuary is one of Griggy's favorite hands. Be aware though, if your opponents get to know your preferred hands, they could make collecting them very difficult!

Sparrow Sanctuary scores well but is a Semi-Concealed Hand, so you may just have to watch as, an essential, One of Bamboo gets discarded. Then. You may have to switch to try for the All Pair Jade (page 68) or All Pair Ruby Jade (page 64) hand.

HANDS OF GOOD FORTUNE

In all games of chance, there has to be an element of luck. In Mahjong, three hands rely on more than a little luck to be able to complete them. Two of these involve being dealt complete or very nearly complete hands right from the start.

Don't expect any of these hands to appear very frequently, in fact; Heavenly Paradise (page 71) is so rare that few players ever get to see one and, at time of writing, I have yet to be dealt a complete Mah Jong from the outset as is required for Earth's Grace (Page 73).

However, being aware that these hands exist is wise; it would be a great shame not to recognize and claim an exceptionally good fortune hand, should it come your way!

Good Fortune Hand

Heavenly Paradise - Ultimate Hand

Calling Mah Jong with this hand will win you the entire game! But it demands a great deal... A Bouquet of Flowers (1-4 of the same colour), a Pung or Kong of Red, White and Green Dragons, plus a Pung of Your Wind and a Pair of any Wind.
For the Fishing scores, the Bouquet does not also count seperately. A Bouquet always scores 1000 (500 2-Player game) except when Fishing for this hand.

HEAVENLY PARADISE

The only hand that requires a Bouquet (either red or black). Also required are Pungs or Kongs of all three Dragons (which score 1000 on their own if you fail to complete this hand, don't have a Bouquet and are not Fishing for a single flower – See Fishing scores above). Finally, to complete this hand, you need a Pung of your Wind and a Pair of any Wind. Odds of getting this hand are very slim, however, if you get a Bouquet or three of the same color flower, early in the round and have Winds and Dragons in your hand, give it a go. The rewards for Fishing are very good.

Good Fortune Hand

Griggy's New
43
Heaven's Grace
UNIVERSAL

MAH JONG 2000

2-Player 1000

Fishing N/A

HEAVEN'S GRACE

FULLY CONCEALED HAND

EAST WIND
INSTANT
MAH JONG!

Only the East Wind player starts with 14 tiles. Just imagine, instead of choosing which tile to discard, you discover that you already have a complete Mah Jong!
It can be any hand as long as it is complete. If so, as well as being exceptionally lucky, you must also declaire Mah Jong before play starts. Heaven's Grace scores 2000 regardless of the value of the hand you have been gifted.

HEAVEN'S GRACE

Heaven's Grace is not a hand that you collect. To claim this, you have to be *East* and have the amazing good fortune to start the game with a complete hand.

Very rarely does this happen, but East should always check their hand before discarding their first tile. Once that first tile is discarded, this hand cannot be claimed.

Good Fortune Hand

Griggy's New

44

Earth's Grace

UNIVERSAL

MAH JONG
2000

2-Player
1000

Fishing
N/A

EARTH'S GRACE

INSTANT SUCESSFUL FISHING HAND!

Any player, except the East Wind

SEMI-CONCEALED HAND

You pick up your initial 13 tiles and discover you are Fishing so need just one tile to call Mah Jong. That's very lucky but you have to be extra lucky to win Earth's Grace... You must complete the hand (any hand) when you pick up your very first tile (either from the wall, discard or loose tile after picking up a flower. Earth's Grace Scores 2000 regardless of the value of the hand you complete.

EARTH'S GRACE

You are indeed lucky if you start the game Fishing. However, to also claim Earth's Grace, you must first declare that you are Fishing and then complete the hand with your very first tile. Earth's Grace can be any hand, but will always score either 2000 in a four-player or 1000 in a two-player game.

SCORING ADDITIONAL HANDS

In Griggy's New Universal, there are forty-four hands. The vast majority of these are traditional Mahjong hands that were collated by Max Robertson, and others, in the 1960s. Griggy, herself added Red Arrow (Page 49) and Round Table (Page53) was my contribution.

When first introduced to this game, I will freely admit to being very apprehensive about the large number of hands I would need to learn, or at least understand. Creating this guide and the hand cards have certainly helped not just me but others new to Mahjong. However, when talking to players and searching online, I was disturbed to find that hundreds more have been created over the last two decades. One player insisted that there were two hundred and fifty hands that all should be included in this guide.

During further research, I discovered that some of these new hands were not possible without using wild cards (Jokers) and that many others presented the same fourteen tiles in a different pattern, along with a new name and different score. Clearly, this is both illogical and impractical. Including them would only serve to disinterest another generation of potential players.

As stated at the beginning of this guide, we wanted to make the game easier to play and more inclusive. Adding over a hundred new hands would defeat this aim. However, Griggy and I may not have included your favorite hand and who are we to say you can't continue to use it? The only problem you face is how to score it so that it compares with the forty-four in this guide. For that reason, I include the scoring formula (see next page) which was used to calculate the scores printed on the hand cards and forms the basis for the hand card scoring system.

Griggy's Universal "Mah Jong!" Hand Scoring Calculator

ELEMENTS: Applied to each element in the hand

KONG (or requirement for two Pairs of the same tile)	+500
PUNG - Purity Suit, Wind or Dragon	+300
PUNG - Mixed Suits hand	+200
PAIR or CHOW	+200
SINGLE RUN of 1 to 7	+500
TWO RUNS of 1 to 7 (total)	+1400
RUN of 1 to 9	+1000
RUN of 2 to 8	+800
ONE OF EACH Wind or Dragon PLUS EXTRA of any	+400
ONE OF EACH Wind or Dragon without Pair	+300

HAND REDUCTIONS: Deducted from Hand Total once.

Where Dragons or Winds have replaced Kongs or Pungs	-600
Mixed Suit Pairs are used (as in Knitting)	-200
Mix Suit Tri's are used (as in Tripple Knitting)	-300

HAND BONUSES: Applied to Hand Total

PUNG/KONG of all three Dragons	+1000
Bamboo Colour Specified*	+400
Odd or Even Numbers Specified	+400
Honours (1's and 9's) Specified	+400
Wind Pairs Specified	+400
Concealed Hand Required **	+600
Final tile must be from wall***	+600

*Except where both colours are required.
**Does not apply to Buried Treasure Hands.
*** Applies only if it is a requirement for the final tile to come from the loose tiles or a specific tile is the final tile on the wall.

The scoring guide is only needed to score any additional hands you wish to add to the game. It is not required for any other purpose. Its sole use is to derive a score or a Fishing score, from a hand that is not included in Griggy' Universal as standard

Some adjustments have been made to certain hands to balance minor irregularities discovered during test games.

MAHJONG Q&A

This final section was nearly given the title 'Everything Else.' Because I am aware that certain minor issues are not covered in the earlier sections, mostly because they made the instructions appear too complicated or long-winded. I also include some myth busting that appears within some other guides.

What if more than one player wants a discard?

It is quite possible that more than one player is waiting for the same tile and an argument could break out over who's tile it is. The priority for this is as follows.

A player who can complete a hand and call "Mah Jong!" has priority. If there are two or more players able to call "Mah Jong!" with this tile, then the player to the right of the 'discarder' has priority. i.e., This would be the next player to take a turn if play continued normally in an anti-clockwise direction. In any other situation, the priority is also with the player nearest the right of the discarder.

Speed: Do players have to take their turns quickly?

This is a hang-over from the original Chinese game that only involves only Kongs and Pungs. The Chinese game and can easily be completed very rapidly and the Chinese excel themselves at this.

American Mah Jong is far more difficult and harder to play at such a pace. Certainly, I would advise playing as fast as you are able, but never pressure beginners to play quickly. Mahjong is a game to enjoy, not a sport to race through.

Pairs: Does every Mahjong hand have to include one?

No. This myth has been cut 'n' pasted from an error in an early publication. It *is* true that most hands do include a Pair. However, the traditional hands of both Gertie's Garden (page 44) and Gretta's Garden (page 57), do not.

Can you Abandon a hand?

There will be rounds that just don't go your way. You either see that other players have exposed elements that contain a tile or tiles that you need or these appear among the dead tiles. If it is too late to switch to another hand, then your best course of action is sabotage! Hold onto or collect tiles that may prevent your opponents from completing high-scoring hands. Hanging on to Winds, Dragons, and Honours Bamboo tiles are often wise choices. Also, look at any exposed elements your opponents have made. Holding on to tiles of the same suit may scupper their ambitions.

PENALTIES

New players, in particular, may find they have too many or too few tiles in their rack, (or have this pointed out to them). This is usually a mistake caused by either forgetting to discard or by forgetting to pick up a Loose Tile after picking up a flower or making a Kong. They may also call a false "Mah Jong!".

While there should be penalties for these errors, the penalty should not ruin the round.

Having too few tiles

There is no advantage in having too few tiles, so the penalty is minor: The offending player must miss two turns during which time they cannot pick up a discard. After missing two turns, they should pick up a Loose Tile before taking their turn.

Having too many tiles

This is more serious because a player with too many tiles has an unfair advantage. The player must first lose a random tile or tiles to make it right. They may shuffle their rack before that player opposite picks the extra tile (or tiles) from the offender's concealed rack. These are then treated as discards with the other players able to call for them. The offending player then also misses two turns without being able to pick up any discards.

Calling "Mah Jong!" in error

If a player calls "Mah Jong!" and either they or the other players recognize the error before they start to expose their tiles, the penalty is less severe: They must leave their hand displayed to the other players and continue to play to the end of the round with their tiles all exposed. A Buried Treasure bonus can't be claimed even should they manage to call "Mah Jong!"

If any of the other players have started to expose their hands in response to the false call, then the penalty is more severe because the round has to be called void. The offending player loses 500 Points, and all the other players each receive 500 Points. *EAST* retains the title and Marked Rack even if he was the offending player.

Playing out of turn

Often a result of an impatient player, someone may take tiles from the wall or even a previous discard before the last player has discarded and ended their turn. If not the player 'in play', you should not be touching any tiles except those in your own rack. By doing so, you may be hurrying or distracting another player.

It is important that those waiting their turn do not start moving tiles from the wall, or the discards in advance of their turn. This behaviour is distracting and can confuse beginners. Once warned, any player repeating this misdemeanour should miss their turn.

A request from your Authors

We hope you were able to follow the instructions in this guide and can now begin to master and enjoy Mahjong. We are particularly interested in getting feedback from new players, for whom this guide is aimed. If you have returned to the game after failing to grasp it from another manual, then please let us know.

If you struggled with any section or found our explanations difficult, please tell us. We can try to rectify this or anything else in future editions.

Veteran players: We know any new manual is going to cause some conflict with those playing any of the many other variants of the game. However, we still want to hear from you. Apart from gambling – which we are never going to include, is there anything you would add? What is your favorite hand and have we included it?

richardweston247@gmail.com

We value all feedback; A one-star review with valid explanation will serve us just as well as a glowing five-star review.

Many Thanks,

Richard T Weston and Pauline Day

Other books by Richard T Weston

Turf Wars Ingleton Manor (1st Limited Edition copy is SOLD OUT)

When Life Deals you Melons – Writing with Dyslexia – eBook / Kindle only. Available from Amazon

Murray Weston a Life through Poems – eBook / Kindle only. Available from Amazon

Guide to Zen Gardening – Free online article rt-print.co

Contents

Erratum and update history:

V1.00 Hand No.24 'Odd Characters' Buried Treasre option text included in error. Removed from v1.01

V1.02 following requests from users, a 4-player score card has added at the end of book (Page 84)

NOTES:

Quick look-up SCORE CARD

Page	Hand	4 Player Score
24 -	ORDINARY SUIT HAND	1000
25 -	PURITY SUIT HAND	1400
26 -	ALL HONOURS HAND	1800
27 -	ALL KONG HAND	2000
28 -	WRIGGLY SNAKE	1400
29 -	DRAGONFLY	1100
30 -	CHINESE ODDS	1800
31 -	KNITTING PAIRS	1000
32 -	TRIPPLE KNITTING	1000
33 -	ALL PAIR HAND	1400
34 -	ALL PAIR HONOURS	1800
35 -	WINDY CHOWS	1000
36 -	HEAVENLY TWINS	1400
37 -	UNIQUE WONDER	1500
38 -	WINDY ONES	1400
39 -	WINDY NINES	1400
40 -	GATES OF HEAVEN	1800
41 -	A RUN, A PUNG AND A PAIR	1500
42 -	HEADS AND TAILS	1400
43 -	RED LANTERN	1100
44 -	GERTIE'S GARDEN	1400
45 -	MIXED PUNG HAND	1200

Page	Hand	4 Player Score
47 -	LOST SOULS	2200
48 -	ODD CHARACTERS	2400
49 -	RED ARROW	1500
51 -	PLUCKING PLUMB BLOSSOM – ROOF	3000
52 -	PLUCKING THE MOON - SEA BED	3000
53 -	THE ROUND TABLE	1800
56 -	ALL WIND AND DRAGON	1400
57 -	GRETTA'S GARDEN	1100
58 -	THE THREE GREAT SCHOLARS	1700
59 -	WINDY DRAGONS	1800
60 -	THE FOUR BLESSINGS	2000
62 -	RED LILY	1800
63 -	RUBY JADE HAND	1800
64 -	ALL PAIR RUBY JADE	1400
65 -	LILY OF THE VALLEY	1800
66 -	ROYAL RUBY	1800
67 -	IMPERIAL JADE	1800
68 -	ALL PAIR JADE	1900
69 -	SPARROW SANCTUARY	1900
71 -	HEAVENLY PARADISE	WINS GAME!
72 -	HEAVEN'S GRACE	2000
73 -	EARTH'S GRACE	2000

www.ingramcontent.com/pod-product-compliance
Lightning Source LLC
Chambersburg PA
CBHW060820270326
41930CB00003B/98